I0418406

IT AIN'T ROCKET SCIENCE, FRIEND!

How to Position Your Expertise, Build An Authentic Personal Brand, and Plan a Profitable Launch in 90 Days.

By

Brianca Johnson Kirkman, M.A.

Brianca Johnson Kirkman. © 2022

All rights reserved. No part of this book may be reproduced, stored, or transmitted by any means- whether auditory, graphic, mechanical, or electronic- without written permission of both publisher and author, except in the case of brief excerpts used in critical articles and certain other noncommercial uses permitted by copyright law. Unauthorized reproduction of any part of this work is illegal and is punishable by law.

ISBN: 979-8-9873415-0-6

ISBN E-Book: 979-8-9873415-2-0

Because of the dynamic nature of the internet, any web addresses or links contained in this book may have changed since publication and may no longer be valid. The views expressed in this work are solely those of the author and do not necessarily reflect the views of the publisher, and the publisher disclaims any responsibility for them.

Cover Design: Ashlee Nicole of Artistry Studios

Photo: Mecca Gamble of Mecca Gamble Photography

Editors: Dr. Joel Boyce of JCB Educational Services

For more information, please visit:

www.briancajohnson.com

Visit briancajohnson.com/book-resources

For free resources to help you position your expertise, build an authentic personal brand, and plan a profitable launch in 90 days.

Printed in the United States of America

For the hidden-gems.
May the strategies in this book help you position
yourself as the in-demand expert
who I know you are.

TABLE OF CONTENTS

INTRODUCTION

Welcome to *It Ain't Rocket Science, Friend! A 10-Step Framework to Position Your Expertise, Build an Authentic Personal Brand, and Plan a Profitable Launch in 90 Days* and thank you for purchasing this book.

If you are reading this book, then I know you have a proven expertise that you are ready to monetize. You are overwhelmed and frustrated with the steps to make that happen. Every now and then, you bang out content or send an email to your list, but you've struggled to build momentum because you have no idea what you should be executing on a day-to-day basis. You're watching YouTube videos and implementing quick tips here and there, but the pieces still aren't clicking.

You probably feel like an imposter and doubt that you actually can make money from your skills and expertise. Sure, you've seen others do it, but you can't figure out how to make it happen for yourself.

I wrote this book to show you that you CAN build an authentic personal brand and make money from your expertise, even if you don't have a large following and can't commit to posting everyday. It can happen; you just need some easy-to-imple-ment, no-fluff strategies you can execute without overwhelm or overthinking.

I never wanted to be an entrepreneur. It took me a very long time to see my business as an actual business, and because of this, I spent many years as the expert who no one knew – a hidden-gem. The strategies that I'm going to cover in this book helped me and so many clients like me transition from being a hidden-gem to an in-demand expert.

Since 2014 when I first started my business as a blog called "The Life and Times of Bree," I've helped hundreds of women start and grow businesses that leverage their expertise. Initially, my goal was to document growing my business and entering the world of work, but over time, it evolved. I began taking on clients, helping them with social media, email marketing, web design, and so many other digitally-related things in between. Although I was a beginner, and I was just starting to get the hang of it, I always have had a very strategic brain. Because of that, my clients were seeing results even from the beginning. I was able to leverage these results to position my expertise and attract more of my ideal clients.

At the time, one of my clients was running to be a State Senator, and he ended up winning. I talked a lot about the work that I did on that campaign – designing the website and logo and building out the social media strategy, etc. This was right as I was graduating with my master's degree in Marketing and Advertising Communications from Webster University, so I really wanted to leverage this experience and my results to pivot my career into digital marketing and move out of St. Louis.

A friend reached out to let me know that she knew of someone who was looking for a digital director in Atlanta, Georgia. I had never even been to Atlanta, but I was desperate for a job, so I applied. Within 11 days, I'd accepted the position and moved across the country to begin work as the digital director for the Democratic Party of Georgia.

I had no family or friends in Atlanta. I was taking a job in a political environment about which I knew nothing and working on a campaign for one of the most influential political personalities in history (not debatable). At the time, I had no idea what I was about to do, but it was one of the most challenging and rewarding seasons of my life. It set the foundation for every blessing and opportunity that has transpired since.

In this book, you'll learn more about how I built a multi-six-figure business teaching women entrepreneurs easy-to-implement, no-fluff marketing strategies, so they can leverage their expertise to build profitable businesses and design a harmonious life. It is my prayer that by the time you finish reading this book, you will have the clarity and the confidence you need to execute. Every strategy that I teach here is one that I've used and taught to my students and clients, so I know they will deliver results if you do the work.

Before we dive in, it's important that you understand a few things:

1. Marketing is not one-size-fits all.

I'm going to teach you basic strategies and tactics in this book, but it is up to you to put your own spin on it. What works for one business owner may not work the same for you depending on your audience, your brand personality, or brand voice.

Your job is to consider the strategies taught here and decide how to implement them while remaining authentic to yourself, your audience, and your business.

2. Marketing is all about momentum.

It's very easy to get discouraged when you aren't seeing the results that you desire, but marketing is all about momentum. The second you give up, you'll have to start over with gaining your audience's trust and priming them to purchase from you. It's important that you see your plans through til the end once you begin executing. You never know who is going to make the decision to work with you because you sent one more email, posted one more time, or sent one more text message. Don't give up.

3. Test, Assess, Repeat.

As you start implementing strategies, think of them as mini experiments. Your job is to execute the strategy, review and assess the results, optimize, and then run it again. As I stated, marketing is all about momentum, so the more you test your strategies, the better equipped you'll be to optimize them and start converting more clients in shorter periods of time.

Now, you're ready to dive in and begin positioning your expertise, building an authentic personal brand, and planning a profitable launch.

Client Case Study:

Name: Jance Chartae

Business Name: The Boutique Academy

Website URL: https://www.theboutiqueacademy.com/

Facebook Page:
https://www.facebook.com/theboutiqueacademy19

Instagram:
https://www.instagram.com/theboutiqueacademy/

Tell us about your business. Who do you serve and what do you do?

The Boutique Academy is an online school for boutique owners and e-commerce brands who want to learn how to build profitable online stores.

What was your biggest struggle with marketing before working with Brianca?

My biggest struggle was that I had plenty of ideas and I thrived in creativity, but I don't thrive in processes and organization.

What has been your biggest lesson since working with Brianca?

The biggest lesson I've learned since working with Brianca has been that it's okay to not try to accomplish all things at one time. However, I can find a creative and organized way to do all the things I want to do with structure and a plan that supports my goals.

What advice would you have for an entrepreneur just learning to market?

I would tell an entrepreneur who is just learning to market that understanding your audience or ideal client always will make marketing easier. If you truly understand them, you'll know exactly how to best serve them through your marketing. Your words and actions always will make sense with your audience who are at the forefront of your decisions.

CHAPTER 1:
A Profitable Vision.

Once the campaign was over, I realized that I'd put my business on the shelf. I hadn't been talking to clients, promoting my services, or even documenting my experiences in my role. Since work was slowing down, I knew I was ready to pivot and get back into my business, so I decided to take on work as a consultant – this was the beginning of me getting paid for my expertise.

I launched a done-for-you marketing service that allowed me to operate as a fractal chief marketing officer for my clients. I helped them clarify their messaging, so they could get in front of their ideal clients, develop marketing campaigns, and build automated marketing systems, so they could grow their business on autopilot – basically the exact same work that I was doing as digital director on the political campaign.

I knew that if I wanted to take my business to the next level this time around, I had to get very clear about what I was building. I needed to understand who it was that I wanted to serve and why I wanted to serve them, and I needed to be clear about the best way for me to serve them. We'll talk a lot about this when we discuss unique positioning, but I wanted to be sure that I stood out in my industry, and I was building a sustainable business.

I identified my profitable vision for my business by outlining my overall mission, vision, and values. I knew that this would serve as a decision-making compass for me, but I also knew that my mission, vision, and values would be reflected in my brand at every touch point – from our emails to our content to the programs and services that we offer. For these reasons, I knew that it was important that I get this right and take it seriously.

Mission

Your mission is the "why" behind the work that you do. You also can identify your mission by considering the thing that you want to change in the world or your environment. Think of it as the reason that your business even exists. Your mission statement should be one to two sentences long and identify:

- What you do
- Who you do it for
- Why you do it

Here's our mission statement:

To provide easy-to-implement, no-fluff marketing strategies for coaches, consultants, and CEOs across the world.

Vision

Your vision statement is where you see your business in the next five to ten years. This is basically how your business would look if you achieved all your goals. As you're identifying your vision statement, consider:

- How do you want to be viewed in your industry?
- How big or small do you want your team to be?
- How does your work/life balance look?
- What kind of clients do you select?
- What products and/or services do you offer?

Here's our vision statement:

To provide over 1,000,000 coaches, consultants, entrepreneurs, and professionals with the clarity and confidence to execute profitable marketing campaigns and build automated marketing systems through teaching, consulting, and implementing digital products.

If you get confused while writing your mission and vision statements, think of it this way. Your vision is where you're headed, and your mission is what you need to be doing now to get there.

Values

To keep it simple, your values are what you believe. Your values most often are reflected in the way that you communicate with your clients and serve them.

Here are our values:

- Excellence + Integrity
- Master Strategy Through Innovation
- Village (Community)

- Planned Action

- Seen, Served, & Safe

- Authenticity + Individuality

Most people skip over this step of identifying their mission, vision, and values, or they don't take it seriously, but that's problematic. Your mission, vision, and values will serve as a compass for your decision-making. There have been a number of times when I felt myself making decisions based on what was happening in my environment or in the industry and I've had to reference my mission, vision, and values to check myself and get back on track.

Every decision that you make should be evaluated from the lens of "is this getting me closer to my vision or taking me further away." If the work you're doing is getting you further away from your vision, then you know that it is time to stop, assess, and recalibrate.

It's important to note that your vision can change and evolve. As you grow and learn new things, you may want something entirely new or different for yourself and your business, and that's ok. However, if that happens, be sure to write out what your new mission, vision, and values are, so you know exactly what you're working towards.

Take Fast Action:
Complete the mission, vision, & values companion exercise in your book bonus portal at
https://www.briancajohnson.com/book-resources.

Client Case Study:

Name: Rosalind Flemming

Business Name:

Facebook Page:

Instagram:

Tell us about your business. Who do you serve and what do you do?

I am an education consultant who trains school principals, executive directors, and mid-level school leaders to retain Black staff. I also provide coaching and strategic planning to school leaders to help them retain Black teachers.

What was your biggest struggle with marketing before working with Brianca?

My biggest struggle is not being clear about my offers, pricing, and target audience.

What has been your biggest lesson since working with Brianca?

My biggest accomplishment is gaining clarity of what I seek to do, what my promise is, and what my brand identity is.

What advice would you have for an entrepreneur just learning to market?

My biggest advice for an entrepreneur who is just learning to market is to invest in yourself. We do these posts and reach out to people, but we may not understand what we are doing. It is important to reach out for help because marketing is the next big step after you've established your business. I have seen how marketing has supported my brand and how I am being known in my community as an advocate for Black teachers and leaders.

CHAPTER 2:

Your Secret Sauce

At the very top of 2021, I relaunched my business as Brianca Johnson & Company. I'd spent the better part of a decade before this period building a persona that was the watered down, more palatable version of me. I changed my name, wore different hairstyles , covered up my tattoos, and selected noteworthy clothes in my photoshoots. I learned how to water myself down and fit in to get ahead, and it worked while I was in corporate America, but when I decided to go out on my own, I knew I needed to do it authentically.

This meant allowing myself to be vulnerable and transparent, so my audience could make a genuine connection with me. When you're first starting out in your business, nine times out of ten, your ideal clients are who you used to be. You're able to place yourself in their shoes and speak to where they are in their lives or business because you've been there. It's your job to connect your expertise and experiences to the transformation that you'll provide.

At the time that I was relaunching and trying to grow this business, everybody and their mama were on the internet, and they were trying to coach or grow a business. Not only did I have to deliver results, but also I had to stand out from competition. I knew the only way to do this was to understand my industry and my competitors.

Your competitors are business owners who provide the same or similar service to the same or similar audience as you.

Here's the thing. If you know why your customers prefer working with or purchasing from your competitors, you know what to address in your messaging. The absolute best way to identify this is through a SWOT Analysis. SWOT is an acronym that stands for strengths, weaknesses, opportunities, and threats.

By conducting a SWOT analysis, you're able to utilize internal and external data to build profitable marketing strategies and identify your competitive advantage. In a SWOT analysis, strengths and weaknesses are based on internal data and opportunities, and threats are based on external data. Here's a breakdown:

- **Strengths** - What are you doing better than your competition?

- **Weaknesses** - What is your competition doing better than you?

- **Opportunities** - What is happening in your industry or environment that is working in your favor?

- **Threats** - What is happening in your industry or environment that is working against you?

Here's an example based on a company that sells digital planners. We'll call them Planning Pals:

- **Strengths** - Planning Pals provides tutorials and training on how to use their planners for optimal success.

- **Weaknesses** - Planning Pals is not leveraging TikTok to highlight their products or build a relationship with their audience.

- **Opportunities** - Apple is releasing a new iPad that will make it easier for beginners to access digital planners.

- **Threats** - There's a campaign to limit screen time on devices.

Based on this SWOT Analysis, Planning Pals would be able to alter their marketing strategies to create TikTok tutorials that highlight how their customers can use their digital planners with the new Apple update. They'd also be able to share public facing tutorials to their online audience about how to use digital planners. Lastly, as a result of this SWOT Analysis, Planning Pals could create a campaign that documents how users of their planners spend less time on their devices aimlessly scrolling because they are more efficient with their time.

The benefit of conducting a SWOT analysis is that it allows you a bird's eye view of your position in the market, but it doesn't allow you the opportunity to assess how your competitors are positioned. To understand your competitors, you'll need to conduct competitive research.

Competitive research simply is identifying your competitors and conducting a SWOT analysis on them.

Here are the steps to conduct competitive research:

1. Identify your competitors.

You can identify your competitors by considering:

- With whom do your ideal clients work instead of working with you?

- To whom do your ideal clients look for trusted information outside your business?

- With whom do your ideal clients work before they work with you?

2. Analyze their online presence.

You should visit their website and social media profiles and review any press features they've done. You want to understand:

- How do they identify themselves?

- What service/products do they offer?

- How often do they post on social media, write blogs, or get published in newsletters?

- What topics do they discuss most frequently?

- How engaged is their audience?

3. Gather information.

As you're visiting their website and social media, you should be gathering information.

- Download their lead magnet.

- Subscribe to their email newsletter.

- Join their free community if they have one.

- Ask yourself:

- How many emails do you receive and what's the messaging?

Your job is to engage with their brand at as many touch points as possible because you want to know:

- How do they communicate and engage with their audience?
- What's their buying/enrollment process?

4. Conduct a SWOT Analysis.

Using the information that you've gathered while conducting your competitive research, it's time to complete a SWOT analysis on your competitors.

- **Strengths** - What are your competitors doing better than you?
- **Weaknesses** - What are you doing better than your competitors?
- **Opportunities** - What is happening in your industry or environment that is working in your competitors' favor?
- **Threats** - What is happening in your industry or environment that is working against your competitors?

By conducting a SWOT analysis for your business and your competitors, you are better able to identify market gaps and opportunities.

A market gap presents when your ideal clients have a need that is not being filled by you or your competitors.

Upon completion of these exercises, you should have identified clear pathways to improve your business or messaging or optimize your marketing to build a deeper connection with your ideal clients. You also should have a better understanding of your secret sauce – what makes you stand out from your competitors.

It's important to note that these exercises should not be completed one time and then put on the shelf, never to be looked at again. Your job is to remain abreast of what your competitors are doing and what's happening in your industry. Here are some strategies for you to put in place to make sure that happens:

1. Turn on Google Alerts for your business and yourself.

    a. What are people saying about you?

    b. Do you see any trends?

    c. How do these messages fit into your SWOT Analysis?

2. Turn on Google Alerts for your competitors.

    a. What are people saying about your competitors?

    b. Do you see any trends?

    c. How do these messages fit into your competitive research and the SWOT Analysis you conducted on your competitors?

3. Create a folder in your email to save your competitors' emails.

    a. Are they addressing any pain points in their messaging that you currently are not?

    b. Are they addressing any desires in their messaging that you currently are not?

    c. Are their subject lines more or less engaging?

    d. Based on their emails, is there anything that you should add or take away from your email marketing strategy to be more effective?

4. Conduct competitive research on a quarterly basis and before launching new offers or products.

Take Fast Action:

Complete the SWOT analysis exercise in your book bonus portal at
https://www.briancajohnson.com/book-resources.

CHAPTER 3:

Unique Positioning

N ot being able to articulate your value can cost you confidence, clients, and coins.

When I first decided to go full-time in 2020, I had a number of clients whom I was serving as a fractal marketing consultant. I knew that in order to scale my business, so I could replace my salary, I'd have to be able to serve more clients without spending more time. I decided that I would do this by teaching more small business owners how to market their business.

At this time, I hadn't yet built up an audience online. My business was growing steadily through word-of-mouth advertising, but I was not positioned properly as a marketing coach. I basically was starting from scratch, but I didn't see it that way because I'd been working in marketing roles for so long, and I already had a book of clients. I naively thought that my expertise would just translate, and clients would be knocking down my door to work with me. I was wrong.

In 2020, I had my first failed launch using a webinar strategy. I hosted a free 90-minute webinar for small business owners, coaches, and consultants who wanted to learn how to build profitable marketing campaigns. The problem was that my audience didn't even know what marketing campaigns were at the time and they definitely did not trust me to teach them to build one. Why would they?

- I hadn't spent any time talking about my work as a digital director.

- I failed to share or highlight campaign successes that I had in my work.

- I'd completely let my personal brand and business fall to the wayside when I moved to Atlanta.

All of these things led to zero enrollment from my webinar to my courses. However, this was the beginning of me positioning myself. I went back to the drawing board to think strategically about why the launch failed, and I realized that I'd missed a key component of the marketing and sales process – I had failed to prime my audience. **Priming your audience is when you spend a dedicated period of time educating your audience about your expertise and building excitement for the offer to come.** Priming your audience easily can be the difference between not hitting your enrollment goal and having a successful five-figure launch.

Even in my role as digital director, we spent a significant amount of time priming our audience, so I knew that it was a critical part of the process, yet I'd skipped it. Couple the fact that I didn't prime my audience, and I wasn't properly positioned as an expert, and you have the recipe for why my launch failed.

I started really talking about this on social media because webinar launch strategies were the bread and butter of a lot of marketing coaches at the time. However, new and beginner entrepreneurs weren't seeing a lot of success with the strategy for the same reasons that I wasn't successful – they weren't positioned properly as experts in their industry, and they hadn't spent enough time priming their audience. As a side effect of these failed launches, I was seeing too many qualified coaches and consultants feeling discouraged and unmotivated. They were lacking confidence in their business, and I wanted to help.

I started sharing more about why my launch failed, why it happened, and how I was able to begin having five-figure launches more regularly using my signature three part framework: *Position Your Expertise, Prime Your Audience, and Plan Your Launch.* I also started being vocal about how much I hated webinars and how ridiculous I thought it was to sell a one-size-fits-all approach to marketing. My audience began connecting with my message and trusting me as an expert.

They resonated with this message because it was an authentic part of my experience as an entrepreneur who really just was getting her foot in the door with growing an online audience. I made it clear that just because you're new to growing your business doesn't mean you're new to delivering results as an expert. This was key, especially since I didn't even have an established audience online when I tried to host my first webinar. I had to increase my brand's visibility by sharing my expertise, positioning myself, and talking about the work that I did in my career and the ways it aligned with the services that I offered to my clients.

Your unique positioning is how you standout in your industry and what sets you apart from your competitors. It's based on your value and the transformation that you provide, while highlighting key elements of your personality, values, beliefs, and strategic insight. Refer back to your SWOT analysis if you are having trouble establishing this.

To help identify your unique positioning, you can use the 5P framework:

1. **Position** - What are you the very best at doing?

2. **Person** - Whom do you want to serve? Why do you want to serve them?

3. **Proof** - What qualifies you to serve? Where did you learn or gather the skills/expertise to serve them?

4. **Process** - How do you solve your ideal client's pain points? This is your framework or the steps that you teach repeatedly to help your clients get results.

5. **Promise** - What transformation will your service help them receive?

Once you answer these five questions, you can use this framework to put it all together to create your positioning statement:

Here is the framework for identifying your positioning statement: "I <POSITION> <PERSON> to <PROOF> THROUGH <PROCESS> so they can <PROMISE>."

Example: *I teach coaches and online service providers how to position their expertise, prime their audience, and plan their first 5-figure launch.*

As a result of getting clear about my unique positioning, I've been able to identify my target audience, clarify my messaging, and refine my offers. This has led to an increase in my audience size, revenue, and speaking engagements. My audience now knows me for portions of my marketing like my "Marketing Muva" tagline, my belief that marketing is not a one-size-fits-all approach, and the fact that I don't think new entrepreneurs without a proper audience should launch using a webinar strategy.

Your goal is to identify what you want your audience to know you for.

Take Fast Action:
Complete the positioning questions exercise in your book bonus portal at
https://www.briancajohnson.com/book-resources.

Client Case Study:

Name: Lenae Meyers

Business Name: The Virtual Nae

Facebook Page: https://www.facebook.com/thevirtualnae

Instagram: https://www.instagram.com/thevirtualnae/

Tell us about your business, who do you serve & what do you do:

I am a productivity coach who helps female entrepreneurs combat burnout and overwhelm by managing their energy, so they can live a life of ease.

What was your biggest struggle with marketing before working with Brianca?

My biggest struggle before the course was getting clear on my launch plan when it comes to leveraging my audience online.

What has been your biggest lesson since working with Brianca?

My biggest lesson would be leveraging my current clients/audience by using what previously has worked for past clients to serve them.

What advice would you have for an entrepreneur just learning to market?

Document everything including feedback from clients or any feedback or comments you receive from posts. You can use that to leverage content ideas or build it inside your program.

CHAPTER 4:

Your Ideal Client Avatar

The riches are in the niches.

- Unknown

When you're first starting out, it always seems like a good idea to broaden the scope of your marketing to include anyone who possibly could benefit from your services. This is a mistake. Your marketing should be segmented, targeted, and positioned to an ideal client. It will save you time, marketing dollars, and headaches.

As I was relaunching my business and focusing on consulting, I had no idea with whom I wanted to work. This led to me just taking on new clients without really being sure that they were a good fit. Being a good fit doesn't just mean that they operate in the industry you serve, or they pay the invoice on time. It also may mean that they have the tools, resources, mentality, and infrastructure to execute what you teach them. It's also just as important that they respect your boundaries and honor deadlines and processes.

Your job as a business owner is to be crystal clear about who you best serve. This ideal client should be in alignment with your experience, expertise, and promised transformations. One way to identify your ideal client is to create an ideal client avatar (ICA). An ideal client avatar is a character who you create based on the details and information that you know about whom you best serve.

By diving deep and understanding your ICA, you're better able to target your marketing to seek out more qualified leads instead of attracting larger quantities of leads who are not a good fit for your business.

You can create your ideal client avatar by identifying a past client with whom you've worked who was a best fit, or you can create your ideal client avatar by identifying someone in your network who would be the best fit for your services and building your avatar based on what you know about them.

Here are some of the questions you should be answering when building your ICA:

- What is my ideal client's name?
- How old are they?
- What do they do for a living?
- Are they married?
- Do they have kids?
- What is their biggest pain point when it comes to <your expertise>?
- Why is this pain point a headache for them?
- What have they tried before that didn't work?

- Where do they seek out trusted information?

- By alleviating this pain point in their life, what transformation will they experience in their life or business?

- What is the deeper motivator pushing them to have this pain point alleviated?

Using these questions as a foundation, here is an example ideal client avatar:

Simone is a 29 year old residential advisor at a four year university in Massachusetts. Simone is in a committed relationship and lives with her significant other while they save to pay off debt and purchase a home. As a side hustle, Simone writes and reviews resumes for corporate women of color (WOC) who want to pivot their career. Simone believes that WOC should have peace, joy, and ease in the balance between their career and their home life, and they should be fairly compensated for the work that they do. Simone also believes that many WOC professionals are too humble on their resumes, and that's why they don't stand out. Simone has seen a great impact from her resume review services and wants to build out a coaching program tailored to WOC professionals who want to advance their careers in higher education. Simone's biggest struggles with building this program are a lack of knowledge around building out the curriculum, marketing the program, and launching it to her ideal clients. She has followed marketing coaches, listened to podcasts, and read books to increase her knowledge, but she is ready for a 1:1 coaching experience to get her program launched. Simone knows that if she is able to launch and grow her coaching business, she will be able to grow her side hustle, quit her corporate job, and experience more financial and time freedom in her life. Simone wants to experience more luxury, travel more, and build generational wealth for her family and siblings.

Using this ICA, I'd be able to target more ideal clients with similar demographics, interests, and pain points as Simone.

Your ICA is not something that you write one time and then forget about. It's important to think of your ICA as a compass that leads you to the right people at the right time. However, in order for this to happen, your destination always has to be up to date. This means you should optimize your ideal client avatar continuously based on what you learn about the clients with whom you work. You also can gather this information on a recurring basis by including questions like these on your application or discovery form:

- What is the most pressing issue happening in your life or business right now?

- What have you tried already to resolve this problem that didn't work?

- Why are you applying to work with me?

- What made you decide that now is the best time to move forward?

- How would you like to see your life or business transformed after working with me?

When used in your marketing, the answers to these questions will help you strengthen your messaging and convert more clients in a shorter time period because you'll be able to speak directly to them.

As your business grows, you may see that you have a different client avatar for each of the offers in your business. This is normal. Your offers may speak to similar clients, but at different stages of their journey, which means you need different messaging. As you are building out your ICA, consider your customers' journeys and how you want them to move through your business. This will help you identify which offers in your business need their own ICA.

Take Fast Action:
Complete the ideal client avatar exercise in your book bonus portal at
https://www.briancajohnson.com/book-resources.

CHAPTER 5:
Bridge of Connection:

In 2020 when I decided that I wanted to go full-time in my business, I hosted my first webinar, and it failed. I'd been operating from a "build it and they will come" mindset, but that's not how marketing works, and I knew that. I started thinking about how I would have marketed my webinar if I had been doing it in my corporate role, and I immediately understood what I did wrong. I was trying to sell before I positioned myself or the offer properly.

Basically, I'd broken the rules. I just showed up one day and started trying to get my audience of college friends and family to pay me. They weren't even my ideal clients, but I ignored that because I didn't trust myself. I thought that what I knew about marketing wouldn't apply as an entrepreneur, but once I realized that I was wrong, and I understood my corporate expertise actually would make my entrepreneurial journey better, I began implementing a real strategy.

I started talking about this failed webinar experience. I'd recognized that so many new entrepreneurs were having the same problem – wasting a bunch of time building a webinar launch without properly positioning themselves and then feeling discouraged and frustrated when it failed. Leveraging my corporate expertise, I began sharing strategies online for these entrepreneurs to position themselves as the expert, prime their audience with their offer, and profitably plan their launch (my signature framework).

This was the turning point. I began seeing my audience and revenue grow. When building an authentic personal brand and platform, it's important to build a bridge of connection between you and your audience. You want them to see you as an expert, but you also want them to build a meaningful relationship with you, and this comes from knowing your mission, vision, values, and story which we talked about in chapter one. However, it's important that you share your failures, mistakes, and the lessons learned because it allows your ideal clients to see you as human and connect your story and your transformation with where they currently are and where they desire to be.

One way to do this is through our core brand stories.

Core brand stories are the stories from which your business and platform are built. You share these stories often in your content and marketing. Typically, these stories are the building blocks of your relationship with your audience, and they create a bridge of connection.

The best brands are the ones to which we feel an emotional connection. This is especially true when building a personal brand.

Here's an example using one of my core brand stories.

In 2020, I was working as a digital director for a national nonprofit. At the time, I was working close to 80 hours per week as a salaried employee (meaning I wasn't being compensated for my nearly double *workload), and I was exhausted. When the COVID-19 pandemic hit, and I was forced to sit at home and really reflect on my life, I knew that things had to change. I decided that the best way to change my circumstances was to increase the revenue that I was generating in my business and get 3 new fractal CMO clients. I'd previously tried to host a webinar to get the clients that I needed, but I wasn't properly positioned in my industry as an expert. Instead, I started reaching out to current clients, informing them of my new package, and talking more about marketing, my expertise, and the results that I'd delivered. I got the clients, and on July 1st, 2020, I resigned from my role as digital director and went full-time in my business. That year, Brianca Johnson & Company generated its first six figures, and I helped my top 6 clients generate over $260,000.*

This is a story I tell all the time because my clients are primarily corporate professionals who are overworked and underpaid. They desire to replace their corporate salary with their business and quit their job to be full-time in their business. This core brand story allows them to see that I was once in their shoes, and it provides an opportunity for me to share how I reached the transformation they desire using my signature framework – positioning my expertise, priming my audience, and planning a five-figure launch.

Your core brand story should share your story while highlighting your framework as the key to alleviating their pain points and achieving their desires. You can craft your core brand stories by answering these questions:

1. What was the pain point you were experiencing?

2. How did you feel as it was happening?

3. What steps did you take to alleviate the pain point and achieve the transformation you desired? (*Your framework or expertise.*)

4. Did you experience any setbacks or roadblocks along the way? (*Their objections*)

5. As a result of implementing these steps, what happened? (*Their desires*)

As a guiding principle, I recommend that you have 3-5 core brand stories that you use to connect with your audience. They can be developed from common pain points or desires, but they should highlight your framework or expertise clearly as the vehicle for change.

Take Fast Action:

Complete the bridge of connection exercise in your book bonus portal at
https://www.briancajohnson.com/book-resources.

CHAPTER 6:
Collecting & Sharing Receipts

Men lie. Women lie, but numbers never lie.

When I found out I was pregnant in 2021 with my son Brayden, I decided that I wanted to go back to corporate America. Essentially, I wanted to create more structure in my life without worrying about working around the clock while I navigated learning how to be a mom. With this decision, I hired my friend and career coach to help me update my resume and stand out while I was looking for the perfect position.

It was during this process that I was tasked to speak about my expertise and the impact that it has had for my students and clients. I knew that I'd served hundreds of people, but I didn't know exactly how many, so I started digging. After looking through my customer relationship management software, Stripe portal, contracts, and more, I realized that I'd served over 500 students and clients. I couldn't believe it.

One of the most overlooked and underused marketing tools is data. Being able to speak to your expertise using quantitative and qualitative data points is often how you can close the gap with potential clients. However, it's also how you can boost your confidence when first starting out, starting over, or pivoting.

There are two types of data that you should be leveraging in your messaging and marketing - quantitative and qualitative data.

Quantitative data is data that has a numerical value.

Qualitative data is data that describes qualities or characteristics.

As you're positioning yourself, you want to be sure that you consistently are collecting data that speaks to the impact that you've had with clients, the results that you've driven, and the ways your clients felt while working with you.

Questions you can ask to gather quantitative data:

- As a result of working with me, how much money did you make?

- In what time frame were you able to see results after applying strategies I taught.

- On a scale of 1-5, with 5 being excellent, how would you rate your experience in the program?

Questions you can ask to gather qualitative data:

- Having completed the program, how do you feel about <subject matter>.

- What would you say to someone who's on the fence about working with me?

- What was the most impactful thing that you learned while working with me?

It's important that you consistently are capturing both qualitative and quantitative data in order to position yourself as the expert and speak to the value of your program or service on a regular basis. I also want to note that you can collect this data at various stages in your customers' journeys. It does not have to only be done at the end of a service.

Here are some strategies to capture data continuously:

1. You can capture data that speaks to where a client is before working with you by aggregating the data in your onboarding forms and applications.

2. You can capture data that speaks to the shift in your clients perspectives while working with you by offering a middle-of-the-course check-in. This check-in can be as simple as a repeat of the questions asked during onboarding or the application process.

3. Of course, you can capture data that speaks to the overall transformation that your clients have by asking questions at the end of a service.

If you have a Facebook group, or you attached a community to your programs or services, I recommend creating a Google drive folder where you can house testimonials. Organize the folder by offer and then by month and year. Example: *Clarity to Coins*, May 2022. As students share their wins or breakthroughs in the community, you can screenshot them and save them to this folder, so you always will be able to access and reference them.

The more opportunities that you provide for your clients or students to talk about their experience while working with you and the transformation that they have, the better and more holistic data sets you'll have.

This information can be used continuously to position you as an expert by sharing it online with your audience, but it also can help you grow your business by analyzing the trends.

1. Is there anything that your clients feel they need to know before or after working with you that is aligned with your expertise?

2. Are there any improvements that your clients feel would make their customer experience better?

3. Are your clients speaking to you or your programs in a way that you have not, and could make your transformation clearer for your ideal clients?

It's one thing to collect the data continuously, but you also have to analyze the data and make improvements continuously to your messaging, marketing, or offers based on the trends that you identify. You can easily identify trends by compiling your data and testimonials in one Google sheet or document and highlighting words or phrases that you see repeating.

The biggest lesson that I learned when I went full-time in my business in 2020 is that it doesn't matter how good you are if no one knows it. Until that point, I'd struggled with talking about my work as a digital director. I'd built and launched digital marketing campaigns and marketing systems for national political campaigns and nonprofits across the country, yet I refused to talk about it because I felt like it was braggadocious to share my wins.

This flawed way of thinking was actually the number one thing holding me back and preventing my ideal clients from seeing me as an expert. Sharing your impact is about building trust with your audience by showing your track record of results. It's one thing to have systems in place to capture qualitative and quantitative data, but you also have to have systems in place to share the data that you collect. This is where most people fall short, but that won't be you because you're reading this book.

Depending on the type of data that you collect, qualitative or quantitative – different methods of sharing can be more or less effective.

Quantitative data is best shared visually with graphs, charts, or screenshots.

Qualitative data is best shared from the clients' own perspectives and words through written or video content.

When both qualitative and quantitative data are present, I've found case studies to be the most effective way to share my impact. A case study is simply the process of recording your student or client's results over a period of time. Case studies are most effective when you have both quantitative and qualitative data.

Here are the questions you can ask to capture the information for your case study:

1. What were you struggling with before working with me?

2. What strategies did you deploy to help your clients overcome their challenges?

3. What results were achieved?

4. What do they have to say about their experience working with you?

The easiest way to capture a case study is by scheduling a 1:1 interview, recording the call, and transcribing the recording. This also will allow you the opportunity to repurpose the content in a variety of ways such as:

- Reels
- Video Clips
- Tweet graphics
- Quote graphics
- Blog Posts

Take Fast Action:

Complete the case studies exercise in your book bonus portal at
https://www.briancajohnson.com/book-resources.

CHAPTER 7:
Expert Content System

As you're building your personal brand, it's important that you create content that positions your expertise. This means creating content that answers your ideal client's most pressing questions, provides solutions to their problems, showcases your results and transformations, and educates your client about your framework. It's about more than just jumping on Instagram trends or dancing in reels. It's about positioning your profile as a resource and go-to for your ideal clients.

One of the biggest mistakes I see new entrepreneurs make is getting caught up in the content hamster wheel. They feel like they have to churn out new ideas and strategies constantly to keep up with constantly changing social media platforms. Instead, they should be creating a system of content that is built off repurposing and repositioning content.

As I was preparing for maternity leave, I started thinking through my content strategy. I knew that I wanted to generate sales in my business consistently while I was out, which meant that I needed to create content that had a longer shelf life – podcasts, blog posts, and YouTube videos. I also knew that I needed to leverage SEO in my content, so I could get Google to work for me and drive leads to my website even when I wasn't promoting my offers actively.

This meant that I needed to build an expert content system. This system is my method for creating one core piece of content and repurposing it across multiple platforms. Before you can leverage this system, you have to be clear about where you want your business to show up. Here are examples of platforms that you can choose:

Platforms You Own:

- Blog
- Podcast
- Newsletter

Social Media Platforms:

- Instagram
- Twitter
- Facebook
- LinkedIn
- YouTube

I recommend starting with 2-3 platforms, being sure that at minimum, one of the platforms is owned by you. Here are some popular examples to get you started:

- Blog & Instagram
- Podcast & Twitter
- Blog, Newsletter, & Instagram

Once you've identified the platforms you want to leverage, you then need to identify how many times per week you want to post on each platform. This will help you identify how many pieces of content you need.

Example:

1. My primary platform is: Blog

   a. I will share one blog per week.

2. My secondary platforms are Instagram and LinkedIn.

   b. I will post on Instagram five times per week.

   c. I will post on LinkedIn three times per week.

3. In total, I need 9 pieces of content each week.

Now that you've gotten clarity about how many pieces of content you need, it's time to build out your expert content system.

1. Identify 12 keywords for which you want to be known. These will be your content topics.

In order to benefit the most from SEO, you need your website and content to populate in search results when people are searching for answers to their questions. As an example, when people search for *"positioning statement,"* I want my business to pop up in the search results because I talk about positioning your expertise as part of my signature framework.

2. Using those keywords, map out the answers and resource content you will create.

Once you've identified the keywords for which you want to be known, you can use tools like Keywords Everywhere and Answer the Public to identify questions that are being asked around those keywords. Identify one question for each piece of content that you need.

As an example, I know that I need nine pieces of content, and when I search "positioning statement" in Answer the Public, I see 56 questions that are being asked online. Some of these questions might be duplicates, or they just may not make sense for the content that I am creating, so I narrow those 56 questions down to these key questions that I can answer.

- What is a positioning statement?
- What is the purpose of a positioning statement?
- What should a positioning statement include?
- What is an example of a positioning statement?
- What is my positioning statement?
- How long should a positioning statement be?
- Where do I publicize my positioning statement?

You may not find the exact number of questions that you need for the total number of posts that you want to share, and that's ok. You can cross promote content and even repurpose or reposition content as part of your expert content system. Example: Although I wasn't able to find nine quality questions using Answer the Public, I know that I can repurpose content from the answers to the questions that I did find and create additional content like quote graphics, tweet graphics, examples, and testimonials.

3. Post on your primary platform.

Now that you've identified your 12 content topics, you have weekly content themes for the next 12 weeks. It just has to be repurposed down into multiple content pieces. The first step is to create one longform piece of content and share it on your primary platform. I recommend that your primary platform should be a platform that you like such as a blog, podcast, or newsletter.

In your primary content, you want to provide answers to all of the questions that you found, being sure to incorporate your keyword.

As an additional framework, I recommend being sure that your primary content also answers these questions:

1. What is the topic?
2. Why does the topic matter to your ideal clients?
3. What are 3-5 key talking points for the topic?
4. What is a story, strategy, or transformation related to the topic?

Example: Positioning Statement

1. Define what a positioning statement is.
2. Include a story about how I used my positioning statement to pitch myself as a speaker for a conference.
3. Share with readers what are the 5 P's of positioning statements, how you can craft your positioning statement, what are some examples of positioning statements, and when you should share your positioning statement.

4. Present how using my positioning statement in my pitch resulted in being booked as an expert speaker for 5 conferences.

4. Repurpose for secondary platforms.

Once your longform piece of content has been completed, you can create repurposed content using your primary post as a foundation.

You can share:

- A story related to the key topic

- A strategy related to the key topic

- A transformation you've delivered using a strategy related to the key topic

- Compilation of your 3-5 key talking points

- A quote from the longform content

- A live based on a topic in the longform content

- A feedback or testimonial related to the key topic

Using this framework, you'll be able to create content consistently that positions your expertise without having to create new content every single day.

> **Take Fast Action:**
> Complete the content planning exercise in your book bonus portal at
> https://www.briancajohnson.com/book-resources.

CHAPTER 8:
Profitable Platforms

B uilding an expert content system is one way to position your expertise and launch an authentic personal brand, but it's also important that you increase your visibility by penetrating new audiences where your ideal clients are.

When I launched the Marketing Masters Implementation Lab, I knew that if I wanted to hit my goals, I'd have to get in front of more of my ideal clients which meant leveraging profitable platforms.

Profitable Platforms are platforms that you do not own, but they target your ideal clients. You can identify your profitable platforms by looking to complementary experts, podcasts, and publications that your ideal clients see as a trusted resource.

By identifying my profitable platforms, I was able to begin pitching podcasts that targeted my ideal clients by creating a mini podcast tour. This podcast tour, along with my subsequent promotion of each episode, resulted in an additional $750.00 per month in recurring income. This example speaks to the power of leveraging your profitable platforms to expand your brand reach and visibility.

Increasing the number of people who know of and interact with your brand is extremely important when it comes to lead generation and conversion.

Complementary experts

Complementary experts are service providers, coaches, or consultants who offer services related to your expertise, but they are not your direct competitors. With complementary experts, you typically are targeting the same ideal client avatar, but for different reasons.

Example: If you are a web designer, a complementary expert for you might be a copywriter who specializes in writing copy for new websites or rebrands.

To identify your complimentary experts, you need to know:

- With whom do your clients work before they come to you?

- With whom do your clients work after they come to you?

- Is there someone who fills a gap with your ideal clients that you don't?

Once you've identified your complimentary experts, you can pitch them for collaboration opportunities like speaking or guest training on their platforms, bringing them in as a speaker or guest trainer on your platform, providing them with an affiliate link and commission, or hosting joint workshops or training with them.

Whether you bring them on your platform or pitch to be on their platform, working with complimentary service providers can grow your audience.

Pitching

Another way to position your expertise and launch an authentic personal brand using profitable platforms is by pitching. Pitching allows you to increase your exposure with your ideal clients through already established platforms.

In order for pitching to work, you'll need to conduct research on the best platforms to reach your ideal client.

1. To what podcasts, magazines, newsletters do your ideal clients subscribe?

2. Who is the point of contact for each platform?

It's a good idea to ask your audience using polls and question stickers who they're listening to, what they're reading, and what events they're planning to attend. Document their answers and use this as a running list of platforms to pitch if they align with your brand and mission.

Once you've identified key platforms to pitch, it's time to set your goals:

1. How many new profitable platforms do you want to be on per quarter?

2. How many profitable platforms do you need to pitch each week to hit this goal?

You can also leverage a tool like HARO (Help a reporter out) to increase your visibility. HARO sends daily emails with links to answer questions from reporters at local and national publications. By replying to the questions with your answers, you could be featured in these publications, thereby positioning your expertise and expanding your reach.

Getting on the profitable platform is important, but the work doesn't stop there. Once you've started booking podcasts, securing speaking opportunities, or getting featured, you have to amplify that content.

Here are some ways you can amplify your features:

- Create a speaking page on your website and update regularly with all of your features.

- Promote your upcoming feature on your social media and to your newsletter.

- Share a recap of your guest training or speaking experience.

- Pull clips from podcast episodes and share on social media.

- Share behind-the-scenes content.

- Repurpose content from your presentation into content on your social media platforms.

Be sure that you don't miss any features by setting up Google alerts for your name and the name of your business like we discussed in chapter two.

Take Fast Action:
Complete the profitable platforms exercise in your book bonus portal at
https://www.briancajohnson.com/book-resources.

Client Case Study:

Name: Qiana Solomon

Business Name: The Virtual Key

Website URL: https://thevirtualkey.net

Facebook Page: https://www.facebook.com/thevirtualkey

Instagram: https://www.instagram.com/the_virtualkey/

Tell us about your business. Who do you serve, and what do you do?

I help photographers organize, streamline, and scale their business with efficient systems and automation in place, so they can work less and focus more on their craft. I specialize in setting up CRM (client relationship management) tools such as Honeybook, 17Hats, and Sprout Studio within 24-48 hours.

What was your biggest struggle with marketing before working with Brianca?

I'm not a marketer. My background is in criminal justice and even as a first-generation business owner, I had to learn about business first. I would show up online. I would launch offers blindly not knowing the missing piece of the puzzle was that I did not have a true marketing strategy to help me reach the right audience and craft the message I needed to convey. Learning about the actual psychology and strategies behind marketing and sales was something that was non-existent for me, but Brianca teaches it in a way that is digestible and easy to implement.

What has been your biggest lesson since working with Brianca?

Know your numbers and collect your data to speak to the work that you put into your business. Analyzing your numbers and collecting the data that you need to support your offers will confirm that the central focus of your business is what your client actually needs, so you don't waste your time. You can design a business that feels good to you, and if you set up your marketing strategy once, you can rinse and repeat if it is done the right way.

What advice would you have for an entrepreneur just learning to market?

Before you invest in anything when it comes to your business, invest in learning how to market your business. You don't want to be years down the road wondering what you are doing wrong and why you are not hitting the goals you desire to achieve. Be clear or at least have some idea of the person with whom you want to work and the capacity in which you want to work with that person. Be open-minded to learn something new and apply what you have learned. It may be trial and error to see what works and what does not work, but stay consistent.

CHAPTER 9:

Packaging Your Expertise Into a Sellable Offer

As you see momentum from positioning your expertise and launching your authentic personal brand, it'll be time to package your expertise into a sellable offer. It is best to deliver amazing results with one offer and become known for it before you begin introducing multiple offers to your ideal clients. The momentum from marketing and mastering one offer will help you position and sell the others.

When I first went full-time in my business, I started as a consultant. I was coming into my clients' businesses and operating as a fractal CMO. I offered this service for the majority of 2020 until I decided that I wanted to package what I'd learned into a group coaching program for online service providers and coaches, which was called Clarity to Coins. You can learn more about Clarity to Coins by visiting www.briancajohnson.com/course

Clarity to Coins is the premier self-paced course and community for emerging entrepreneurs, coaches, and consultants who want a step-by-step gameplan to create your offer and launch it in 90 days or less. The framework for this program is a compilation of the strategies I used to grow my business online alongside strategies I've leveraged in my corporate career. In this chapter, you'll learn how to package your expertise into a sellable offer, so you can begin profiting from your authentic platform.

Clarifying Your Offer

The first step in packaging your expertise is to identify the common problem thread that you solve for your ideal clients. Think back to the questions that are asked via email or DM on social media: what are people constantly asking you for your help?

Once you've identified your common problem thread, you want to outline the structure of your offer. Here are some questions to consider:

- Will it be done-for-you, done-with-you, or done-by-you?
- How long will you work with clients?
- As a result of working with you, what transformation will your clients receive?
- What will be included in your offer?
- How will you describe your offer?
- What will be the name of your offer?

Here are some examples of services that you can offer based on whether it is done-for you, done-with-you, or done-by you:

- ☐ **Done-For-You Service**
  - ☐ Brand/Web Design
  - ☐ Implementation

- ☐ Photography
- ☐ Graphic Design
- ☐ **Done-With-You Service**
  - ☐ Intensive
  - ☐ VIP Day
  - ☐ Group Program
  - ☐ 1:1 Coaching
- ☐ **Do-It-Yourself Service**
  - ☐ Course
  - ☐ Workbook
  - ☐ Template Shop

The more clarity that you have around your offer, the better your messaging and your marketing will be for that offer. It's also important that you're able to speak to how that transformation will be delivered. This is where your transformative framework comes in.

Your Transformative Framework

Your transformative framework is the steps that you take and teach your clients to take in order to achieve the promise of your offer.

As an example, my transformative framework is to position your expertise, prime your audience, and plan your launch. Even this book is written based on that framework. Your transformative framework is often the steps that you took to see transformation, and they may also be based on your mistakes, lessons learned, and hindsight. As you're thinking about your transformative framework, you'll need to consider:

1. The promised transformation of your service

2. The steps that your clients need to execute in order to experience that promised transformation

The best way to identify your transformative framework is to reflect back on your journey. When you were in your clients' shoes, what steps did you take to experience transformation? Take it a step further and look at the clients you've served or consulted with and identify the steps that they took based on your recommendation. Are there any steps that you see recurring with each client? These will be the steps that make up your transformative framework, but it's important that you test out your transformative framework to ensure that it delivers the desired results.

- Are there any steps that you've left out?

- Are there any steps that need to be removed?

- Can any of the steps be grouped together?

When people execute the steps outlined in your transformative framework, what results do they typically experience? What roadblocks or objections do they have? You will want to note the answers to these questions and speak to them in your content. These questions also will give you insight into any improvements you may need to make in your curriculum or with your services.

Your Curriculum

If you have a coaching program, it will be important to overlay your transformative framework over a curriculum. Your curriculum will be the outline that you use to teach. For each step in your transformative framework, you should answer the following eight questions:

1. Your Transformative Framework Step.

   a. **Learning Objectives** - What will students know and be able to do at the end of this lesson?

   b. **Key Vocabulary** - What words do you want your students to know and understand?

   c. **Pre-work** - Is there anything that your students need to complete before they watch this lesson?

   d. **Criteria For Success** - How will you know this module was taught successfully and understood?

   e. **Guided Practice** - What examples will you cover with your students to help them understand the new material and accomplish the objective?

   f. **Independent Practice** - What task will the students complete on their own to ensure that they know/understand the material and can accomplish the objective?

   g. **Assessment of Mastery** - How will you determine that the students understand the new information and can accomplish the objective?

   h. **Homework** - What will the homework (if any) be before the next session?

Along with these questions, you also want to identify a milestone that the students should accomplish at the end of each lesson. This helps your clients gain momentum and begin to see incremental wins. Incremental wins keep your clients engaged and active in your program. It's also an excellent selling point when marketing your offer.

Your Promise

Now that you are clear about your offer, it's time to create your offer promise. You can use this framework: I will help <ideal client> to <transformation> in <timeframe>.

Example: I will help emerging entrepreneurs, coaches, and consultants create their transformative offer and launch it in 90 days.

The more impactful your promise, the greater the chance you'll have of converting your ideal clients into customers. You want to make sure that your promise is not only in alignment with what you deliver, but also it is desirable to your ideal clients, and they are willing to pay for it.

Pricing Your Sellable Offer

Pricing your offer can be challenging, but it doesn't have to be. One of the biggest mistakes I made when it came to Clarity to Coins was pricing myself out of my market. After the Launch Live Show, I nearly doubled the price of the program. Although it was my biggest launch, my conversion rate was much lower, and I enrolled a fraction of the students who I'd previously enrolled.

The new price didn't align with my audience and the place where they were in their business. This is a common mistake, especially with the pressures of creating high-ticket programs. No matter what, there are some rules you can follow to determine the best price for your offer.

1. Research your industry and competitors.

    a. How long are their programs or services?

    b. What are they offering/not offering in comparison to you?

   c. What is their price point?

   d. What makes your offer more/less valuable than their offer?

2. Identify how much time you will spend executing and serving in your offer.

3. Identify the paid tools, resources, and contractors or coaches you'll need to run your offer.

4. Do you have a launch goal?

   e. How many enrollments do you need to hit this number?

   f. Is it realistic?

Price is also a marketing strategy. While being the cheapest in your industry can serve as a marketing strategy in the short term, it's not an adequate strategy when it comes to building a sustainable business with clients you enjoy. You also want to be careful not to be the most expensive. There is nothing more discouraging than having a continuous stream of leads and a low conversion rate because your clients have to save to work with you. You want your pricing to speak to the value of your offer while still being accessible and attainable.

Be sure to keep your eye on trends in your industry, objections, and conversion rates when identifying your program price or modifying it as this can serve as further guidance.

Take Fast Action:
Complete the signature offer outline exercise in your book bonus portal at
https://www.briancajohnson.com/book-resources.

CHAPTER 10:

Launching Your Signature Offer

———————————

I launched Clarity to Coins three times between October 2020 and December 2021. Each time that I launched, I increased my enrollment numbers, conversion rates, and revenue because I was able to capitalize on the momentum and results from the previous cohort. The more I launched, the better my marketing and my messaging got because I was able to assess what worked, what didn't work, or what could be done better.

Launching your offer is a process that should operate on a cycle: launch, analyze, optimize, and launch again.

Step One: Identify Your Launch Goals

Before you launch, it's important that you identify your launch goals. I recommend using the SMART goal framework to identify your launch goals. SMART is an acronym that stands for:

- **Specific** - What do you want to accomplish?

- **Measurable** - How will you measure your success?

- **Actionable** - What steps will you take to accomplish your goal?

- **Relevant** - Why does this goal matter for your overall business?

- **Timely** - In what time frame will you achieve your goal?

Example of a SMART goal:

1. I will sell 20 tickets to my online course over the next 90 days by promoting it on social and via email, so I can generate $20,000.

When identifying your launch goals, it's also helpful to consider targets versus a rigid number. These targets allow more flexibility in your goal setting. You can leverage the good, better, best framework for identifying these targets in your goal setting.

- Good - This is the minimum goal you could hit and still feel accomplished.

- Better - More than likely, this is where your goal actually sits.

- Best - This target exceeds your goal.

When we know what your goals are, we can assess our efforts better and determine whether we're on target throughout the launch. Divide your launch goal numbers by the number of days you have in your open cart period. This will tell you how many enrollments you should be pushing to reach each day. If you see that during this open cart period you are not hitting your enrollment numbers, it is an indication that you need to begin implementing pivot strategies like increasing your marketing efforts, extending your open cart period, focusing on more visibility, optimizing your sales page, etc.

Step Two: Generating Leads & Marketing to Them

Once you know your launch goals, your next step is to begin leveraging your expert content system and profitable platforms to generate leads.

A lead is an ideal client who has expressed interest in your offer but has not converted into a paying customer, yet.

As you are creating your expert content and showing up on profitable platforms, you want to be driving that traffic to a landing page where people can enter their names and email addresses to continue receiving marketing messages and emails from you.

This is how your lead generation funnel should work.

1. Leads enter their names and email addresses.

2. Leads are tagged in your email marketing platform as "Lead: Name of Source".

3. Leads receive a welcome series and are nurtured to your signature offer.

Until you launch your offer, you should be leveraging your expert content to nurture these leads via email, tell your story, and position your expertise. It is of no use for you to capture these leads and leave them hanging until it's time for you to launch because then, they won't trust you.

Your job is to warm them up to you and basically have them excited and ready to pay for your offer even before you launch.

Step Three: Identify Your Launch Timeline

The biggest mistake that I see my clients make when it comes to launching is that they don't give themselves enough time to prime their audience properly. As a rule, I recommend planning your launch with a minimum of a 90-day lead time. This allows time for you and your team to review any existing assets and update and create new assets if they are needed, test your tech, increase your visibility, generate new leads, and prime your audience for your offer.

When planning your launch timeline you need to identify:

- Waitlist Open Date
- Waitlist Close Date
- Waitlist Enrollment Date
- Waitlist Enrollment Close Cart Date
- Public Open Cart Date
- Public Close Cart Date
- Program Start Date

Step Four: Plan Your Launch Event

Your launch event is an opportunity for you to gather all your ideal clients at one time. During your launch event, you are acknowledging your ideal clients' pain points, speaking to their desires, and highlighting your framework as the method to get them from where they are currently to where they want to be. Your launch event is also when you will dive into the details of your signature offer, its transformation, and the way your ideal clients can sign up.

Types of Launch Events:

- Webinars

- Live Events

- Summits

- Workshops

- Training

- IG Live Series

- Podcast Tours

- Challenge

Hosting a launch event is important because it builds momentum with your audience, rallies them around their problem and your framework, and offers your program as the solution. It is also a good way to get in front of a wider group of people.

As you are building out your launch event, here are some questions that you should consider:

- How does this launch event connect to the offer you are presenting?

- How will you position your expertise during your launch event?

- How will you prime your audience for your offer during your launch event?

- How does this launch event tie into your framework?

Launch a Beta

Launching a beta version of your program is important because it gives you proof of concept. Proof of concept just confirms that there is a market for your offer. Basically, it helps you determine:

- Is there an audience for this offer?

- Are they willing to pay for this offer?

- How much do they think it's worth?

- Do they achieve the promised transformation in the promised time frame?

- Are there any tweaks to the offer that you need to make?

When you launch with a beta program, you offer your program to a smaller group of students at a discounted rate. The goal of the beta program is to capture as much data and feedback as possible. This is what you will use to market your offer when it's time for the actual launch.

The very first time that I launched Clarity to Coins, I launched it as a beta program. I enrolled 5 students, and I documented their progress week over week. When I initially launched the program, it was only 12 weeks, but after receiving their feedback, I extended the length of the program to six months because I saw that many of my students were struggling to complete the program in that timeframe.

The beta launch also gave me a lot of confidence to market and launch my offer properly because I had receipts. I knew that I could deliver a true transformation because I'd already done it before.

Launch Tools

Your launch will be in 5 stages. Let's break them down here:

1. **Lead Generation**- Attracting your ideal clients and entering them into your email marketing.

2. **Lead Nurture and Conversion** - Connecting with your ideal clients through your marketing messages and content, providing all of the necessary information for them to sign up for your offer, and closing them as paying customers.

3. **Client Onboarding** - Integrating the new clients into your service or program.

4. **Client Delight** - Providing all necessary information and resources to serve the clients.

5. **Client Offboarding** - Completing the provided service with the clients and removing them from the service or program.

6. **Client Feedback** - Capturing and sharing qualitative and quantitative feedback.

In each of these stages, there are different tools that you can be using to automate this process and make it more efficient. Here are the common tools that I use in my business:

- Email Marketing
    - ConvertKit
    - ActiveCampaign
    - Kajabi
- CRM (Customer Relationship Manager)
    - Dubsado

- Integrator
  - Zapier
- Checkout Cart
  - ThriveCart
  - Shopify
  - Kajabi
- Project Manager
  - Asana
  - Clickup
- Data Manager
  - Airtable

Step Six: Reflect on Your Launch & Optimize

Because launching is a cycle, it's important to reflect after your launch. Here are some questions to get you started:

- What platforms, vendors, or strategies did you not like during this launch that you'd like to switch?

- Are there any areas of your launch that you want changed to move in a different direction (i.e. challenge instead of free guide)

- What about this launch did you absolutely hate/want to remove from your strategy altogether?

- How has your audience size grown over the course of this launch?

- What were your favorite moments of this launch?

- What didn't you like about this launch?

- Did you receive any feedback about your clients' experience that you can update for later?

- Were you overwhelmed during this launch?

- Did you feel supported during this launch by your community?

- Did you give up at any point during your launch?

Use the answers to these questions to optimize your launch for the future. After each launch, you should feel clearer about your offer and more confident in your messaging and marketing, and there should be an increase in your conversions. Launching your signature offer is so much more than posting a pretty graphic one time on social media. By evaluating the answers to these questions, you will be able to see trends in how you can improve your marketing efforts round after round.

You can learn more about developing a profitable launch strategy in the Clarity to Coins course.

Take Fast Action:
Complete the launch goals exercise in your book bonus portal at
https://www.briancajohnson.com/book-resources.

Client Case Study:

Name: Dr. Angelina Davis

Business Name: Excel at Consulting

Website URL: https://excelatconsulting.com/

Facebook Page:
https://www.facebook.com/DrAngelinaDavis

Instagram:
https://www.instagram.com/drangelinadavis/

Tell us about your business. Who do you serve? What do you do?

My name is Dr. Angelina Davis, and I am a consulting coach, business strategist, and host of the Black Girls Consult TOO! podcast. I help women excel as consultants and build profitable and purposeful business, so they can live the lives they truly desire. I'm on a mission to help as many women as possible, especially women of color, achieve success and longevity in this highly competitive, hypermasculine industry.

What was your biggest struggle with marketing before working with Brianca?

Before working with Brianca, I was not using a multichannel strategy. I didn't have a complete marketing ecosystem or proper segmentation. Now, I know where people are entering into my world, what stage of business they are in, and what their core interests are. This has allowed me to increase my capacity by prioritizing my workflow and the platforms on which I show up. I no longer feel the need to be everywhere at once, and that has made my marketing more effective.

What has been your biggest lesson since working with Brianca?

One of the biggest lessons I learned is the importance of having patience and building momentum. Before Marketing Masters, I was changing my approach frequently. I wasn't being patient enough to determine what was working. If it wasn't working, I did not give enough time to determine how it should be modified or improved before completely changing my approach. When I gained a greater appreciation for timing, placement, testing, and sufficient opportunities to gather data, I saw a significant increase in my email list and qualified lead generation.

What advice would you have for an entrepreneur just learning to market?

My advice for any entrepreneur would be to release yourself from the obligation to follow trends and embrace the variety of ways that you can market your services. At the end of the day, you always will perform best using strategies and tactics that align with your strengths and abilities.

Take Fast Action

Spend the next 90 days implementing the strategies that you learned in this book. It is possible to position your expertise, build an authentic personal brand, and plan a profitable launch in 90 days if you outline a plan and take fast action. Set aside time on your calendar to work through each chapter in this book.

Enlist an accountability partner if it will help you, but get it done. When I first decided I wanted to go full-time in my business, I started meeting with my business bestie every Friday at 10:00 a.m. to discuss our goals for the week, wins, and challenges. That accountability really helped me to stay consistent and move the needle forward in my business.

It will seem overwhelming at times, and you may even get frustrated with the process, but don't give up. The clarity will come from the doing, and the confidence will come from the small wins so celebrate them.

Work on your plan for a minimum of one hour per day to build your consistency. Set aside the time on your calendar right now and set an alarm. Your business isn't something that you can do passively, when you feel like it, or when you have time. You have to make time and see it through till the end if your goal is to grow a successful business that will yield results and impact. Starting now, it's time to start thinking of your business as a priority and the catalyst to the time and financial freedom that you desire. You were created to fulfill a unique purpose on this Earth, but that will not come without hard work and sacrifice.

I say this from experience. The closer that you get to fulfilling your purpose and creating an impact, the more mindset blocks you will experience. Imposter syndrome and fear will creep in. You'll begin to compare and overthink and maybe even to criticize yourself and your work. You'll want to slow down or start over because it's not perfect – don't. Push through and see your launch through to the end. Stick to your plan. Remain disciplined and consistent. Remember that on the other side of your obedience are people who are waiting to be served by you. Don't leave them hanging.

I'm rooting for you always.

EPILOGUE

Whew! You made it to the end of this book. Congratulations, but this is only the beginning. Now, the real work begins. It's time to execute on what you've learned. Don't let the information and resources shared here go to waste. The first step in moving from being the hidden-gem to the in-demand expert who you are is to take action.

Here's a quick recap of everything we covered:

Chapter 1: A Profitable Vision: Identify the mission, vision, and values of your business. Get clear about where you want your business to grow and why.

Chapter 2: Your Secret Sauce: What makes you stand out from the competitors in your industry?

Chapter 3: Unique Positioning: Succinctly speak to your expertise and the transformation that you deliver.

Chapter 4: Your Ideal Client Avatar: Build an avatar of your ideal client and use this to make your marketing and messaging more effective.

Chapter 5: Bridge of Connection: Connect your story and transformation to where your ideal clients are and the change they want to see in their lives or businesses

Chapter 6: Collecting & Sharing Receipts: Capture qualitative and quantitative data from your clients that speaks to the impact you've had in their lives or businesses.

Chapter 7: Expert Content System: Build a system for creating and repurposing content, so you can get out the content hamster wheel.

Chapter 8: Profitable Platforms: Leverage existing platforms that target your ideal clients to grow your visibility and expand your reach.

Chapter 9: Packaging Your Expertise Into a Sellable Offer: Turn your knowledge and expertise into a sellable offer that delivers results.

Chapter 10: Launching Your Signature Offer: Launch your sellable offer and begin profiting from your expertise.

If you actually apply the information and strategies provided in this book along with the bonus resources and templates, you can begin positioning your expertise, building an authentic personal brand, and launching a sellable offer today. These are the exact same strategies that I used to make my first six figures in business, but they are also what we used to help our clients generate multiple six figures collectively.

Don't let this be another book collecting dust on the bookshelf. Instead, think of it as a roadmap and use it daily as you work through your marketing strategies. Take the time to complete the fast action tasks and download your companion materials. You have everything you need to get started.

ABOUT THE AUTHOR

B rianca Johnson Kirkman is a marketing automations strategist and consultant for coaches, consultants, and CEOs. She also speaks and trains in the areas of online entrepreneurship, marketing strategy, and personal development.

Brianca is a graduate of Normandy Senior High School in Saint Louis, Missouri. She then attended the University of Missouri-Saint Louis where she graduated with honors and received a B.A. in Business Administration with a Marketing concentration. Afterwards, she received a M.A. in Marketing and Advertising Communications from Webster University while starting her business as a side hustle. Brianca went on to work as the digital director for a number of national nonprofit organizations and political campaigns across the country.

After a decade of building her career in marketing, Brianca quit her job during the COVID-19 pandemic to go full-time in her business as a marketing strategist and consultant. It was during this transition that Brianca realized her desire to help women entrepreneurs make more money from their expertise by leveraging easy-to-implement, no-fluff marketing strategies to grow their business, similarly to what she'd done.

Brianca is the founder of the Clarity to Coins course, the premier self-paced course and community for emerging entrepreneurs, coaches, and consultants who want a step-by-step game plan to create your offer and launch it in 90 days or less.

She is also the founder of Marketing Masters, an implementation lab program for coaches, consultants, and CEOs who want a step-by-step game plan to build an automated marketing ecosystem so they can make more money in less time.

Through her programs, courses, and digital products, Brianca has served over 500 women entrepreneurs, helping them to execute profitable marketing strategies. Brianca has been featured in VoyageATL, TIME Magazine, Google, and Comcast. Her goal is to make marketing simple, actionable, and automated for entrepreneurs across the globe.

HIRE BRIANCA TO SPEAK AT YOUR EVENT

---

www.briancajohnson.com/speaking

From Hidden-Gem to In-Demand Expert

Positioning Your Expertise Through Content to Attract Your Ideal Clients

Your expertise is valuable – whether you've charged for it before or not. Highlighting the results you've delivered in your content and messaging is important to stand out in a saturated market.

Attendees will learn how to:

1. Connect qualitative and quantitative data back to your story to position you as the expert.

2. Leverage your story to build a bridge of connection with your ideal clients.

3. Create a content system that continuously positions you as the expert.

Mastering Marketing Campaigns

Learn How to Develop a Multi-Channel Marketing
Campaign

A marketing campaign should have one unified theme and message that translates across multiple channels without breaking consistency. Your campaign should be positioned, segmented, and targeted based on the audiences and goals for the platforms you will utilize in your campaign.

Attendees will learn how to:

1. Identify the goal, theme, and assets for their marketing campaign.

2. Identify their primary and secondary content platforms.

3. Identify audiences and goals for each social media.

4. Translate campaign messaging for each platform based on the audience and goals.

Hit Your Targets

Leverage KPIs and Historical Data to Plan Profitable
Launches

Your data provides a narrative about your customers and their purchasing behavior that you can use to shorten your customer's journey. Understanding your key performance indicators and historical data will help you to make messaging and marketing decisions before your launch and in real time.

Attendees will learn:

1. What key performance indicators (KPIs) are and how to identify them in their business.

2. How to capture data regularly for their customers in their marketing process.

3. How to leverage KPIs and historical data to make marketing decisions.

WORK WITH BRIANCA

Access free resources and companion templates.
https://www.briancajohnson.com/book-resources.

Digital products and self-study options:
www.briancajohnson.com/shop

Marketing Masters

An implementation lab program for coaches, consultants, and CEOs who want a step-by-step game plan to build an automated marketing ecosystem so they can make more money in less time.

I love Marketing Masters! It's only been two months for me, but I take pages and pages of notes every training session. Brianca does not hold back. She provides tons of value every single time and amazing marketing strategies to help us get better at marketing. If you haven't mastered marketing, then there's definitely something she can teach you. You need to be a part of this membership.

- Christian

Learn more and get immediate access to this exclusive membership: www.briancajohnson.com/membership

Clarity to Coins Course

Clarity to Coins is the premier self-paced course for emerging entrepreneurs, coaches, and consultants who want a step-by-step game plan to create their offer and launch it in 90 days or less.

I was struggling with EVERYTHING before I joined the Accelerator. Lol. I struggled with online visibility, positioning, and authority, which made it so much harder to attract ideal clients into my signature program. I had never launched a program properly before, so I had no clue what steps to take and what boxes to check. FTC taught me so much more than launching. I now have the knowledge, tools, and resources to show up online confidently and promote my offers knowing it is exactly what my ideal client needs. The mindset shift, though a byproduct of the Accelerator, has been a major game-changer because now I do everything in my business with intention and strategy as a CEO should.

- Nadejiah Towns

Learn more and get immediate access to the Clarity to Coins Course: www.briancajohnson.com/course

www.ingramcontent.com/pod-product-compliance
Lightning Source LLC
Chambersburg PA
CBHW070441130626
46553CB00006B/2269